L.O.V.E.

for Teen Moms

You CAN Still Have
Lives Of Vision & Empowerment

Alicia T. Bowens

L.O.V.E.
for Teen Moms

You CAN Still Have
Lives **O**f **V**ision & **E**mpowerment

Alicia T. Bowens

220 Publishing

Chicago, Illinois
220 Publishing
(A Division of 220 Communications)

Published by 220 Publishing
(A Division of 220 Communications)

PO Box 8186
Chicago, IL 60680-8186

www.220communications.com
www.twitter.com/220publishing

Cover and Interior Design by Julie M. Holloway of
JMHCre8ive.com

ISBN: 978-1-63068-255-2

Printed in the USA

Dedication

This book is dedicated to my sons, Aamir and Jaden, my reason and motivation for writing this book.

Table of Contents

Foreword

My name is Aamir and I am Alicia's first son. My mother had me at 15 years old, so I know how it felt to have a young mother, who was also a single parent. It was hard having a mother so young because she was not able to give me all that I wanted at the time. But at the end, it all came together. I am very proud of my mother and glad she overcame her obstacles.

This book informs you about having a child at a young age, taking care of it while still trying to care for yourself, relationships, college, getting a job, and so much more. Anybody who can relate to this situation or reading just to read, will be greatly informed.

When my mother asked me to write this foreword, I did not know how to respond, but I kindly accepted the challenge, so here I am. I feel like my mother is the perfect person to write this book because she actually experienced all of the events that are discussed in the book.

To conclude this foreword, all I have to say is that I really hope you enjoy reading this book.

Aamir Bowens

Introduction

It was not too long ago that I was a teen mom. However, while writing this book, I decided to watch a few episodes of a reality show about teen moms to try and recall some of the emotions and situations that I had experienced as a teen mom. As I watched, I saw one teen mom struggling with her probation, another mom bouncing in and out of marriage because she was confused about her feelings for her kids' father, and two other moms struggling with having a healthy parental relationship with their kids' fathers after their relationships ended. While the show was entertaining, it only helped me recall the negative emotions – the negative perceptions of being a teen mom and how difficult life can be after having a child at a young age.

As I was completing this book, I heard on the news that New York City had just launched a new anti-teen pregnancy campaign. Posters were draped across the city, displaying images of children and marked with sayings such as, "Dad, you'll be paying to support me for the next 20 years" and, "I'm twice as likely not to graduate high school because you had me as a teen." Once again, more negativity and information about how horrible being a teenage mom *could be.*

While that is how life as a teenage mom *could be,* my purpose for writing this book is to inform you that it is not how life as a teenage mom has to be. I wrote this book to share some of my experiences and provide information and resources in an effort to empower teen moms to not accept the type of life that the statistics and the media say they will have. So, if you were expecting this to be a book touting numbers and statistics on teen pregnancy, then you may as well stop reading now. If you are expecting a drama-filled book telling you how horrible my life was as a teen mom and how I struggled and continue to struggle today, then again, please stop reading now.

As a teenage mother who was able to graduate from high school, go on to earn a college degree as well as two masters degrees, and have a successful career, I want to let teen moms know that success is still possible. As a teen mother whose child has thrived in school, has had the opportunity to visit London, and is now deciding on which college offer to accept, I want to let teen moms know that success is still possible for their children. As a teen mother who has friends and relatives who were also teen mothers and are now successful in life, I want to let teen moms know that neither failure nor mediocrity has to be their new normal. As a teenage mom who succeeded, it is my obligation to provide as much information and resources as I possibly can so that other teen moms can achieve their goals.

By reading this book, I hope that teen moms realize that their path to success still exists, and the only way to achieve it is to make the decision to go after it.

The time is now to encourage and empower teen moms, provide them with the information and resources that they need to succeed, and most importantly, show them L.O.V.E.

1. The Baby's Here, Now What?

"*O*ne more push," said the doctor. I gave one final push. Then I heard it – a small, yet strong cry. "It's a boy," the doctor said. The nurse finished cleaning him off and then placed him in my arms. *Wow, I'm a mom,* I thought to myself. *I have a son. This is my son.* As I looked at him, I immediately felt intense love for this little person that I just brought into the world, and at the same time, sheer terror of the great responsibility of having to raise him into his adulthood. How will I know what to do? What if I mess up?

Never did I imagine that I would be having a child at fifteen. I was an honor student, competed in varsity level sports while being just a freshman, and had a great future ahead of me. How did I get here? In that moment, the reality hit me of how just one wrong decision could affect the rest of your life. The choices that I had made up until that point had placed me right at that moment. How would it affect the plans that I had for my life? I always saw myself growing up and going on to be successful, happy, and living the life of my dreams. How was that going to happen now that I had a baby?

The combination of pain killers, overwhelming emotions, and the delivery, left me extremely tired. The nurse took my son away so that I could rest. The excitement of the day slowly began to wear off; however the uncertainty and fear remained. As I finally started to drift off to sleep, I couldn't help but to think, *what have I just gotten myself into?*

Getting Through the Shock of It All

First, it was the pregnancy that seemed so surreal. I couldn't believe that I was carrying something inside of me that would become a living being – my son. Now he was here and it still seemed unreal. I've held him, kissed him, and watched him as he looked up at me. However, the reality of it all was still sinking in.

Regardless of age, no one is ever fully prepared to be a parent. Being so young, not only was I unprepared, but I was also terrified. This wasn't the type of fear that I was used to. At fifteen, the only fear that I was familiar with was that first day of school fear - the type of fear where you were in a new grade and uncertain of the challenges you faced. Not knowing how you would do in this new level of learning. It was a much easier place where not doing well would only result in poor grades. This new fear was much different. There were so many unknowns involved in caring for a child. If I failed at this, I would impact not only my life, but someone else's. How would I know how to care for my son? How would I know when he is hungry? What if he gets sick? How could I possibly make him happy? How could I teach him right from wrong when I'm still learning it myself?

My mind was filled with so many questions and uncertainty. However, all I could do was use the gifts and knowledge that God gave me and do the best that I could. As time went on, I slowly got the hang of things, and I learned a lot along the way. Being a teenage mom gave me a crash course about sacrifice, learning very quickly who my real friends were, and making adult decisions, all while still growing up and learning about myself.

Alone For the First Time

When I first had my son, the visitors were nonstop. Family and friends were constantly coming by to see him and help me out. Then suddenly, the constant visitors disappeared; the thrill of the new little one was gone. Everyone had gone back to their normal lives and routines, and I was left to deal with caring for my son all by myself. It was now just me and the baby. Raising this child on my own suddenly became very real. What was I going to do? How do they expect me to do this on my own? Was I really ready?

Raising a child is a huge responsibility, and deep down inside I wondered if could really handle it. After all, I was still growing and learning about life myself. Now that I had a child, I would have to make sure that I could teach him right from wrong and how to make good decisions, all while learning how to do so myself. I understood that it would take a lot of sacrifice and planning in order to do it successfully. Therefore, I took things one day at a time. I simplified the big picture for myself – to live a successful and poverty-free life with my son. I knew that obtaining the life that I wanted was still very possible. The challenge was now only with myself. I had to start planning for my future. Going back to school was no longer just an option; it was a priority and a must do if I wanted to create a better life for myself and my son. Just because I now had a child did not mean that I had to give up on my future. I did not want to live a life of poverty, having to struggle to provide for us. Therefore, I needed to focus on getting back on track with my education, and making it through to the next step – graduating from high school and then going on to college.

Going Through the Emotions

Having a baby was a big adjustment for my body. After giving birth, my body had to return back to its normal state. This change caused a dramatic shift in my hormones, which sent me on an emotional rollercoaster. One second I was happy about my new bundle of joy, and the next I was in total fear of being left alone with him. The change in emotions occurred for a few weeks after I gave birth.

If you are experiencing an extreme range of emotions, don't be afraid to share how you are feeling with others. This is a completely normal process that most new mothers experience. Sometimes, sharing how you feel may even help you feel better and allow you to embrace the uncertainty that comes along with motherhood.

If after a few weeks you are still experiencing these mood swings, and instead of getting better they seem to get worse, then you may have what doctors call postpartum depression. However, do not try to diagnose yourself. If you are experiencing strong feelings of regret, depression, and fear, and are isolating yourself from others, seek medical attention. Contact your doctor, as well as someone that you can trust, and let them know the feelings that you are having. The sooner you get the help that you need, the better off you and your baby will be and the quicker you will be able to recover.

Far From a Baby Doll

I remember when I was a little girl; I had a few baby dolls that I used to play with all of the time. However, there was one that was particularly my favorite. Her name was Jessica. She was my favorite doll because I could fill her bottle with water, feed her, and then moments later she would wet her diaper.

I had no idea that just a few years later I would be changing the diapers of a real baby – my own child. My son was far different from a baby doll. He required my attention at all times. Bottle feedings and diaper changes were no longer optional or exciting. I couldn't just put my baby on a shelf and then come back when I felt like it. He cried real tears, needed real food, and demanded my attention. Playtime was over.

The reality of motherhood was a far cry from playing with a doll. Being a mother meant that someone was depending on me to provide for them. My actions would directly impact his life, and it was totally up to me to make sure that the decisions I made about my education and my life were good ones.

Sleep – That Thing I Used To Be Able To Do

As soon as I closed my eyes, he cried. Every two hours in the middle of the night, I found myself getting up to feed him, change him, burp him, and then put him back to sleep. Once I finally got back to sleep, it was time for me to wake up and do it all over again.

Establishing a bedtime routine for my child was very important. Not only was it something that he needed, but it was also something that would benefit me. I knew I would have to go back to school soon, so sleep would be something that I would definitely need to be able to make it through the day.

I began keeping my baby up during the day so that he would sleep a little longer at night. I tried to make his bedtime consistent and easy for him to recognize. When it was close to bedtime, I would dim the lights and turn down the television or radio, which helped him understand that it was time to wind down. When it was finally bedtime, I would turn everything off. Sometimes, he would stay awake, so I would let him just lay there, keeping the lights and TV off, and eventually he would go to sleep. Unfortunately, his sleeping pattern did not adjust until well after I returned to school. However, once it did, I found myself feeling well rested and able to tackle my day.

It's Not Just About Me Anymore

The teenage years are a time where you truly begin to learn about yourself. You learn your likes and dislikes, the type of people you do and don't get along with, and you also start to get an idea of what you want your future to look like. More importantly, you gain more independence. Your parents allow you to go places on your own; you become old enough to work and make money for yourself, and above all, gain driving privileges.

When you are a teenager, it is all about you. You have more freedom to do things when you want, and how you want. Every decision you make, for the most part, is for your own benefit. However, being a teenager with a kid can be quite the challenge.

As a teenage mom, there were many difficult decisions I had to make. There were many events and outings that I wanted to attend, and activities that I wanted to participate in. However, I had to turn down many of them, because they were not in the best interest of my son. Although my family was supportive in helping me raise my son, I still had to make some sacrifices. Being present in my child's life was very critical to his development. Therefore, I had to give up some of my activities so that I had more time for him.

Chapter 1 Review

Points to Consider

♥ Having a baby can be an overwhelming experience that requires much planning and preparation.

♥ Education is the key to ensuring a successful life for you and your child. School must remain a priority before, during, and after your pregnancy.

♥ Your body goes through many physical and emotional changes after having a baby. If these changes become overwhelming, seek professional help immediately.

♥ Caring for a child is a huge responsibility, and should not be taken lightly. There will be some times where you will have to sacrifice participation in activities to care for your child.

♥ Having a child means that every action you take or decision you make will now affect two people – you and your baby. Make wise decisions and act in the best interest of yourself and your child.

Questions to Consider

1. How do you think your life has changed now that you have a child? If you are still pregnant, how do you think your life will change?

2. What plans did you have for your life before learning of your pregnancy? Have those plans changed now? If so, how and why?

3. How will you continue your schooling? Have you made plans to return to school after having your baby, or do you have an alternative plan?

4. What are your plans for caring for your child? Who will care for him/her while you are at school?

L.O.V.E. Activity

♥ Being able to successfully navigate your life after having a baby requires planning. Create a chart with the following headers: Education, Career, Childcare, Income, Other Activities. Write the following headers along the side of the chart: Before Baby, After Baby. Now, fill in the chart with your plans for each of the categories before you became pregnant (before baby) and now that you are pregnant or have your child (after baby). Have any of your plans changed? If so, how did they change? Are there any ways you can plan so that you stay on course with your education or career? What about the other categories?

2. Finding the Support You Need

*M*y family was adamantly against me keeping my child. They knew I was a smart kid who had a successful future ahead, and feared that if I had my child, the chance of me obtaining my dreams would disappear. However, after I gave birth to my son, my family was my greatest support system. My mother, although disabled, was determined to help me raise my child. My grandmother quit her job to help my mom with the baby while I was at school. My little sister would often take him while I was doing homework, and became like a second mom to him. My aunt and uncle were my source of transportation to and from work. Even my other close relatives and friends would chip in from time to time. Although being a teen mom was not easy, having the support of my family made the responsibility a lot easier to handle.

When Family and Friends Aren't Enough

Although I was fortunate to have family and friends who gave me the support I needed, there are some families who may not be as supportive. It is critical to surround yourself with people who will be a support system for you. Always try to surround yourself with people who will be a source of encouragement and information. Limit interaction with negative influences. The company you keep and the people you surround yourself with are key to your success.

Reaching out to other close adults may be necessary if the family's support isn't there. Guidance counselors at your school or the spiritual leaders at your church may be other options for you. Some schools may even have support groups for teen parents or information on outside organizations that may be helpful as well.

Childcare

If you don't have a family member or a close adult that is available to take care of your child while you go to school or work, then finding childcare will be an important task to do.

There are typically three types of childcare: childcare centers, home-based childcare, and in-home childcare. Childcare centers are facilities that offer childcare services. Home-based childcare providers are individuals that offer childcare services out of their home. Finally, in-home childcare providers, often called nannies, provide childcare in your home.

Research your options, and select one that will work best for you and your situation. Interview your potential childcare providers to ensure that they will provide the care that you feel will be best for your child. Some childcare providers also charge based on your income, so be sure to ask about that option as well.

Public Assistance – A *Temporary* Solution

Public Aid, or Public Assistance, was a great help for me, especially during my college years. With my mother being on a fixed income, money was very much restricted in our household. After having my son, I was able to get cash and food assistance from public aid, which helped a lot. When I went off to college, I had my case transferred with me. Having public assistance helped me to not worry about how I was going to put food on the table. However, I knew that I did not want to spend the rest of my life relying on public assistance as a source of income. I did not want to spend a lifetime in poverty, which was the only way to continue to qualify for assistance. Therefore, I set a goal for myself to be off public assistance within a year of graduating from college. I planned to achieve my goal by obtaining a job in my field of study.

For me, the most difficult thing about being on public assistance was the mental transition it took to get off of it. While I was receiving assistance, I often found myself not paying attention to how much items cost when I went grocery shopping. I simply bought what I wanted, regardless of the price. When I began to qualify for less assistance, and then eventually none, it was a shock for me. I was not used to having to budget for food and purchase it with my own money. In a way, it seemed unfair. Although I made too much money to qualify for assistance, it was still barely enough to live off of and care for a child. This transition required me to closely monitor my spending and pay more attention to the costs of items that I purchased.

Chapter 2 Review

Points to Consider

♥ Finding a support system is critical to your success. Reach out to an adult you can trust. Connect with local support groups. Always surround yourself with positive people.

♥ Research your childcare options, and choose one that will work best for you. Be sure to ask about sliding scale, or income-based fees.

♥ Public assistance is a great help, but only a temporary solution. Set goals to succeed and transition off public assistance.

Questions to Consider

1. How supportive was/is your family during and after your pregnancy? Do you have any adults outside of your family that you can rely on?

2. What are your plans for childcare?

3. Are you receiving or planning to apply for public assistance? What is your strategy for getting off of it?

L.O.V.E. Activity

♥ They say it takes a village to raise a child. Identify your "village." Make a list of the people you think you will be able to depend on to help you raise your child. If you don't have a support system, identify the areas that you may need help with, and brainstorm how you can get the assistance that you need.

3. Going Back to School

*A*s I walked down the hallway to my class, I noticed a few looks from the other students – some happy to see me back, others uncomfortable because they did not know what to say.

Returning to high school after being on maternity leave was both comforting and challenging. It felt great to once again be surrounded by my peers. However, I realized that my life was now greatly different from theirs. No longer was my life just about going to school, then coming home and studying. I had a child to care for. They could not relate to that.

Having a child in high school quickly forced me to realize who my real friends were. Many of the friends I used to have no longer associated themselves with me, while others stayed by my side and continued to support me. Regardless of the challenges that I would face throughout the remainder of my high school years, I knew one thing for certain – I had to get through high school and go on to college. I now had someone who was depending on me to provide for him, and I knew that completing my education was one way to assure that I would be able to do so.

Small Sacrifices

Having a child in high school is not the end of the world. However, it will require you to make better decisions about how you spend your time. Typically, high school students are almost always busy. They are usually involved in after school clubs or sports, or are busy hanging out with friends. When you have a child in high school, those things are not as important. Yes, you can still be involved in school activities; however, you must also understand that you cannot spend as much time away from home that you may have once spent.

Before I had my child, I was very active in high school. I ran cross country, played basketball, and ran track. I was also involved in pep club, computer club, and a few other activities. After I had my son, I gave up basketball and participated in fewer club activities. I also picked up a job so that I would have a little extra money to help get things that I needed. I had a lot of support from my family, which helped greatly, but I still understood that my son was my responsibility, and I made sure that I provided for him as much as I could.

Even if you are not involved in many activities at school, there may be some sacrifices that you will have to make, such as cutting down the time you spend watching TV and using the computer or phone. You may have to spend more time studying, or switch your study time around to make time for your baby.

Staying Focused

Managing school, while caring for a child, may at times feel like a balancing act. Because of this, it will be very easy to fall behind in school work. Do not allow yourself to become frustrated. Your hard work will pay off in the end. Just remember your end goal: to be able to comfortably provide for yourself and your child without having to rely on any other type of assistance. Distractions are easy to come by. You may have friends who will try to get you to hang out a little longer than you should, ultimately resulting in being unable to complete the tasks that you had planned for the day. Be aware of the people that you surround yourself with. Make sure you have friends around you who have the same goals as you, and who will push you to get your work done and encourage you when you are feeling overwhelmed.

Looking Forward

As time progresses, you will get used to the routine of managing your school work and taking care of your child. If you haven't started already, now is the time to start your college planning. Whether you plan on attending a large university or a small community college, planning is the key in making your transition from high school to college a much easier process. There are many additional things that you must take into consideration when you have a child and still plan on attending college. The next chapter will walk you through the steps of preparing for college and selecting the best one for you and your child.

Chapter 3 Review

Points to Consider

♥ Returning back to school after having your baby may be difficult. You may lose some friends, and realize the value of other friendships.

♥ After having your baby, some sacrifices may have to be made, such as giving up certain activities and/or adjusting your schedule to make time for baby.

♥ Staying focused is the key to your success. Many people may try to pressure you to do things that may potentially throw you off track with your goals. Stay focused and it will pay off in the long run.

♥ Begin planning now for your future. If you plan to attend college, start your research now.

Questions to Consider

1. What was it like returning to school after having your baby? How did the other students react? How did the teachers react? Did anything change?

2. Were there any activities or sports that you had to give up after having your baby? How did your schedule and study habits change?

3. Do your peers often try to persuade you to do things that you know you should not do? How do you respond? Have you lost any friends because of this?

4. Do you plan on going to college? If so, what colleges are you considering? What majors are you considering?

L.O.V.E. Activity

♥ The earlier you begin to plan for college, the better prepared you will be when the time comes. Visit your guidance counselor to discuss where you are right now. Review your grades with him/her and discuss your options. Let him/her know your desires for your future and discuss ways you can achieve that goal.

♥ If you have not decided to return to school, assess where you are. Is returning to high school still an option? Is pursuing a GED more feasible? What are your education plans after you receive your diploma/GED? Contact your high school and talk to your counselor about returning. If that is not an option, ask them about upcoming GED courses and where/how to get registered for them.

4. Preparing and Applying for College

*W*hen I first began planning for college, I originally wanted to go out of state to a historically black college, or HBCU. However, I opted to stay in state so that I would be closer to my family. The thought of being so far away from my support system was scary to me, and was something that I did not think I would be able to handle on my own. The decision to stay in state immediately narrowed down the list of schools that I was considering.

I went to visit a few in-state schools, which helped me get a better feel of their campus life. After going on a few visits, I narrowed my choices down to two. I applied to both, and they both accepted me.

Narrowing Down the List

Plan, plan, and plan some more. Preparing for college begins in high school. There are so many decisions – in state or out? Community college or university? Public or private? Whatever the case, you have to begin the selection and application process early in order to give yourself the most options. The longer you wait the fewer choices you have available.

Before you begin to choose what colleges you would like to attend, you must first get an idea of what you want to major in. What do you want to be? A doctor? Lawyer? Maybe an entrepreneur? If you have already decided on a career path, then you want to make sure that the colleges you pick have the courses that will equip you with the necessary training and degree required to get the job that you want.

If you are not sure of what your interests are yet, meet with your school counselor to discuss what you like to do, and help you decide on a career/major. Most counselors should be able to provide you with a career assessment test to help you identify where your true interests are.

Another factor in choosing a college is cost. College costs have risen exponentially just within the past decade. If you expect to pay out of pocket for school, then you may want to keep the more cost effective options in mind, like local community colleges. Consider attending one for two years, and then transferring to a university to complete your degree. This will help cut your educational expenses nearly in half. If you do decide to attend community college for the first two years, make sure that the classes you take will transfer over to the university that you plan on attending so you can receive credit for what you have completed, and avoid having to retake courses.

Location is also something to take into consideration. Taking your child away with you to college will add a tremendous responsibility on you. Therefore, you want to make sure that you have all of the support you need to help your college years go as smoothly as possible. If you rely heavily on your family for support, then you may want to consider going to a school that will be near them, or at the most only a few hours away. That way, if you have some serious studying to cram in before finals, you can easily make it home so that the family can babysit for the weekend, if they are willing to, while you pull your all-nighters.

Make sure that the communities surrounding your potential schools have the proper amenities and resources for you and your child. You want to be near affordable daycare centers, and grocery stores within a reasonable distance. If you are planning to stay on campus with your child, make sure that the college offers family housing and find out as early as possible the requirements to obtain housing. In some cases, you may be put on a waiting list due to limited availability.

If you will be living off campus, do your research early for apartments or houses for rent. Find out the costs to rent, what utilities are included, and the deposit that is required. You may also want to find out if they are flexible with students who are depending on financial aid to pay the rent, as well as the length of their leases.

College Visits

When deciding on what college to attend, it is a good idea to visit the college campuses that you are considering attending. Often, you see the college brochure and it gives you a "fluffed-up" idea of the campus and the college life there. However, when you actually go visit the campus, what you saw and read in the brochures is nothing like what you see when you arrive. Moreover, going on a college visit helps you experience the culture of the campus. You want to make sure that you feel comfortable and welcomed there. Keep in mind that you will be there for at least three to six years, depending on the type of institution and the pace in which you learn. Therefore, you want to make sure that the environment and the people you will be surrounding yourself with satisfy your needs, and the community resources available to you and your child are plentiful.

ACT/SAT

The ACT or SAT is a critical test that you must take before being admitted into a college or university. Many colleges use the ACT/SAT score as one of their basis for accepting students into their programs. These tests are usually taken towards the end of your junior year of high school, or the early part of your senior year.

Since the ACT and SAT are both very important tests, it would be wise that you take a preparatory class to help you better prepare and become familiar with what to expect on the exam. Some high schools require students take an ACT or SAT prep class as part of their high school curriculum. Others may offer the course only to a select group of students. If you are not sure about the availability of prep classes at your school, check with your counselor. He or she may be able to guide you in the right direction. You may also want to check with your local community colleges and/or universities, as they sometimes offer these courses as well.

Taking preparatory classes helps increase the chance of you scoring higher on the ACT/SAT. A perfect score on the SAT is 2400. On the ACT it is a 36. The higher you score on the exam, the more colleges you will be eligible for acceptance into, and the more scholarships you may qualify for.

Applying For College

By now, you should have gotten your list of colleges that you are considering attending narrowed down to just a few. Now, it is time to apply.

When applying to colleges, it is easier if you work with your counselor to help you gather all of your necessary paperwork, and keep track of the applications that you have submitted and their processing statuses. Colleges usually have very strict application deadlines; therefore make sure you allow enough time to gather all of the necessary documentation to submit with your application. You also want to make sure you allow extra time for mailing documents that colleges require to be sent by mail, such as your high school transcript.

A new way to submit college applications is via the Common Application website (www.commonapp.org). This site allows you to complete one general application, and then select which schools to send the application to. However, not all schools are listed on the site. Furthermore, some documents are still required to be mailed directly to the school you are applying to.

Financial Aid

Applying for financial aid is another critical step to take in preparation for college. Unless you plan on footing the entire bill yourself, this is one step that you do not want to miss. The name of the application is the Free Application for Federal Student Aid, or FAFSA. The types of funding available are usually grants and loans. A lot of the funds they provide are given out on a first come first serve basis, therefore, the sooner you apply, the more funds there are available for you. The deadline to apply is usually around December or January prior to the fall semester, so you want to be sure to stay on top of this. You can apply for financial aid and get more information online at http://www.fafsa.ed.gov.

Being a student with a child gives you the option to apply for financial aid as an independent student. What that means is that your financial need will be determined by your income and not your parents. Make sure when you complete the application, you fill it out completely.

Otherwise, you may delay the processing of your application, and ultimately, the funding of your education.

When applying for financial aid, make sure that you indicate on the application which colleges you want to receive your financial aid information. That will help to expedite your funding to the appropriate institution that you are planning to attend.

Scholarships

Scholarships are the best way to fund your education without having to worry about accumulating a large amount of debt. Scholarships do not have to be paid back, but they often have very specific criteria that the applicant must meet in order to qualify for the award.

There are many scholarships available for students, but it takes a lot of time and research to find ones that you may qualify for. There are many websites, such as www.scholarships.com and www.fastweb.com that provide a database of available scholarships you can search. Check with the colleges that you are applying to as well as scholarships that they may offer.

Talk to your counselor about scholarships opportunities that you may qualify for. If you are a member of a church or involved in other community organizations, check with them to see if there are any scholarships available.

Housing

Once you've gotten accepted into the college you have applied to, your next step is to research your housing options that are available for you. Since you will have your child with you, you will not be able to stay in the dorms. Therefore, you will have to look into either on-campus family housing or find an apartment off-campus.

If you prefer to stay on campus and family housing is available, you should stop by the rental office of the property to schedule an appointment to take a look at their units and submit an application. If they are too far to make a quick trip, then try calling them and see if you can get the process started via email or fax. Check their website see if they offer virtual tours of the units, or if they can mail you any brochures or pictures of the units that they have available.

If living off-campus is a better option, check the newspaper ads for apartments or houses available to rent. You may also want to check around campus for listings that may not otherwise be posted in the newspapers.

Also, look for any available subsidized housing that may offer a sliding scale for rent, meaning that the cost to rent is dependent on your income.

Sublets are another great option. There may be a student wanting to get out of their lease who may be willing to sublet their apartment out to you until their lease is up. After that point, however, you will have to sign a new lease, and the rent may be slightly higher than what you were paying when you were subletting.

Another thing to take into consideration is the landlord's payment flexibility. If you will be relying strictly on your financial aid to pay your bills, then you should let them know before you sign the lease and make sure that they are willing to accommodate your financial needs by allowing you to pay per semester.

Childcare

One final task to do is to look into the childcare options available for your child. If a childcare facility is the option you are considering, pay them a visit and see what programs they have to offer. Make sure their hours of operation will work with your school and work schedules. Spend some time interviewing the caretakers so that you are comfortable with their skillset and values that they will be teaching your child. Do not forget to ask about sliding scale fees!

Next Step: Getting Through College

If you have taken the steps mentioned, you should be well on your way to a smooth transition into college. Now, your focus will change from getting into college to staying there and making it through to graduation.

Chapter 4 Review

Points to Consider

- ♥ When narrowing down your list of colleges, make sure that they offer your major, and can meet the needs of you and your child. Visit as many colleges as you can so that you can get a true feel for the environment and culture.

- ♥ Spend time preparing for the ACT/SAT. Take as many practice exams before the real one so that you know what type of problems to expect on the test and increase your chance of getting a higher score. If you are not pleased with your score on the real exam, study some more and take it again.

- ♥ Give yourself enough time to gather necessary documentation needed for applying to the colleges of your choice. Do not wait until the last minute.

- ♥ Apply for financial aid early. Remember, the earlier you apply, the more aid you may get.

- ♥ Research scholarships and work with your counselor to identify any scholarships you may qualify for.

♥ Find housing and childcare options that will work best for you and your child. Be sure to ask about sliding scale fees.

Questions to Consider

1. What colleges are you considering attending? Did you visit any of them? If so, were they what you expected?
2. Are you preparing for the ACT/SAT? Does your school offer prep classes for the test?
3. Have you applied for financial aid?
4. Are you researching scholarships? How much time per day do you spend applying?
5. Do you plan to stay on or off campus? What are your housing and childcare options?

L.O.V.E. Activity

♥   Make a list of your college must-haves. What are your
     transportation requirements? What are your housing
     and childcare requirements? Now, make a list of your
     nice-to-haves, the things that you would like but can do
     without. Identify the colleges that meet most of the
     needs on your must-have list. If the list is still too
     broad, go to the nice-to-haves and narrow it down from
     there. How many colleges are left?

5. College: Managing Your Time and Resources

*O*kay, so now I made it to college. As I settled into my new apartment, I couldn't help but to feel overwhelmed about it all. Here I was, finally on my own. Although I was only two hours away from home, it still seemed like I was a whole world away. I was excited and at the same time scared of finally having my independence.

Living off campus had its pros and cons. On the positive side, I did not have to be cramped up in a dorm room with someone that I did not know. I had my own private bathroom. Also, I had a fully functional kitchen, and I could cook whatever and whenever I wanted. On the negative side, by living off campus it was harder for me to meet other new students. I missed establishing those friendships that were usually made in the dorms. I also had to cook, pay bills, and fend for myself. Not to mention, I would soon have my son to take care of (I did not bring him down until two months after I started school). Living off campus, and for the first time being by myself, I often felt lonely and homesick. However, once my son came down and I established a routine for the both of us, I soon got used to it.

Learn Your Surroundings

Whether you have decided to go to a large university, or a community college, take some time to see what the campus, as well as the surrounding communities, have to offer. What organizations or activities are available that you may not have been aware of earlier? Where are the nearby churches that you may consider attending? Where are the grocery stores? Becoming familiar with the area around you will help you settle in and reduce feeling homesick or like you are in a strange land.

Tapping Into Local Resources

If you have not already applied for public assistance, you should take a trip to the local Hunan Services office to apply. While you are working on bettering yourself by obtaining an education, you should take advantage of every form of assistance that is available to you. Your goal is to only receive assistance while you are in school, and then by the time you graduate, you should no longer need or no longer qualify to receive the assistance because ideally, you should be able to obtain a decent paying job to support you and your child once you graduate.

Check around campus for single parent support groups to help you connect with other single parents at your school. It is always helpful to have others to share your experiences and concerns with who can relate to what you are going through.

Scheduling Your Classes

When scheduling your classes, pick class times that will work best for you. Schedule your classes during the time your child is away at daycare, and leave large enough gaps between your last class and the time that you have to pick your child up from daycare so that you have time to study without interruption.

Virtual or online classes may also be a great option. That way, you are free to login whenever you get the chance and can work around your child's schedule.

You also want to schedule your classes so that your workload is not too heavy. Having to divide your time between your studies and your child may not be optimal for a heavy workload, where large amounts of study time are needed. You may have trouble putting in all of the hours needed to keep up with the pace of the classes. Know how much you can handle, and do not worry if this may put you on a five-year graduation plan instead of four. Getting a quality education while caring for your child is what is most important.

Managing Your Time

Learning to manage your time effectively is the key to success in college. Try allocating a time for all of your activities. Get your major studying and errands, such as laundry and grocery shopping, done while your child is at daycare. The sooner you learn to effectively manage your time, the better off you will be when it comes to studying and getting assignments done when they need to be.

Developing Good Study Habits

Every moment you can get to study is a good one. Get in the habit of reading chapters whenever you have a free moment, or have some downtime. If you are not good with studying alone, then invite a few of your classmates over to have regular study sessions. They definitely will not mind coming over, especially if you bribe them with a meal.

If you are having trouble understanding a lesson, make time to meet with the professor or teaching assistant to get clarification. It will be to your advantage to keep lines of communication open between you and your professor or teaching assistant. That will help you establish a relationship with them, which will make it easier for you to communicate with them should any problems arise.

Partying

While studying is very important in order for you to succeed, having some downtime is just as important. It helps you not feel so overwhelmed by the responsibilities that you have. Allow yourself to have a little fun. Find a babysitter, and go out and enjoy the campus with a few other friends. College is all about finding that balance between work and play.

However, you must party responsibly. Know when to stop, and know when it is time to head home. Do not let having fun distract you from what you are supposed to be doing, or keep you from taking care of your responsibilities. Again, the key to being successful in college is learning how to manage your time and prioritize your responsibilities.

Chapter 5 Review

Points to Consider

♥ After making it to campus, take the time to learn your surroundings so that you know what is available to you. Tap into local resources that may benefit you and your child.

♥ The key to being successful in college is learning how to effectively manage your time. While your child is in school or daycare, use that time wisely. Schedule your classes within that timeframe and use that time to get any major reading or studying done.

♥ It is okay to have some fun every now and then. Be sure to use common sense in knowing how much partying is enough. Do not let partying hinder you from taking care of your responsibilities.

Questions to Consider

1. What was it like when you first arrived on campus? What amenities are near you? What community resources are available to you?

2. How can you manage your time to ensure that you get your studying done and other tasks you need to complete?

3. Do you prefer to study at home or somewhere else? How can you fit studying outside of your home into your schedule?

4. How can partying too much affect your schedule? How can you reduce the temptation to party often?

L.O.V.E. Activity

♥ Create a chart with the days of the week as a header for each column. List the hours of the day down the row. Document your daily activities for a week, taking note of what you do and the time that you do those things. At the end of the week, take a look at the chart. Identify the times that you are the most productive. Are there any time wasters that you notice on your chart? Can you incorporate more into your daily routine?

6. Managing Your Money

*H*aving worked in the banking industry, my mom was great at tracking every penny she spent. She would spend hours at a time calculating how much money she had coming in and allocating her money towards the bills, groceries, and other things we needed. Although we lived on a fixed income, people thought we were rich because my mom always had the money to get us the things we needed, and a lot of times, things that we just wanted.

Boy, did I not inherit that habit! While I often saw my mom sit for hours tracking her money, I never grasped the mechanics behind the process. I had it completely mixed up. When I received my refund check, I would pay my rent and car note for the semester, take care of all the bills, and after that, my funds were depleted. I was not regularly attending a church at that time, so tithing was the furthest thing from my mind. My warped definition of saving was that it was something you did only after you paid all of the bills and had nothing else to spend your money on – which often was never. I needed things and began living off of my credit cards. I used them to buy groceries, get gas, and even at times pay for my childcare expenses.

By the second semester of my freshman year, I stopped using my check to pay the bills, and instead, began to go shopping! There began my bad habit of splurging. I would pay a portion of my bills and then buy electronics, clothes, and get my hair done from time to time. The combination of these bad money habits forced me to get a job, fall behind on my bills, and nearly get evicted from my apartment. I ended up with major credit card debt, a large amount of student loans, and bad credit by the time I graduated.

Establishing a Budget

Because you are living on limited funds, it is extremely important that you establish a budget for yourself to ensure that the money you receive will last you throughout the school year. If you are living off of your financial aid and public assistance, allocate your refund check towards paying your rent as far ahead as you can, or at least through the first semester. Put some cash away in a savings account to save for emergencies.

It will be very tempting for you to go out and splurge on shopping with the refund checks that you receive from school. However, if you do so, then where will you get the money to pay your bills? How will you pay the rent? You do not want to risk not being able to pay rent just because you have the urge to buy something new. Practicing responsibility now will help you develop the discipline to better manage your money.

Student Loans

There are two types of loans – subsidized and unsubsidized loans. Subsidized loans do not accumulate interest while the loan is not in repayment status. Unsubsidized loans, on the other hand, do accrue interest.

In the case that you do have to take out loans to pay for your education, try to use them sparingly. Loans can quickly accumulate, and they go into repayment six months after you graduate. Be sure to keep track of how much you are borrowing because you do not want to graduate and then discover that you owe tens of thousands of dollars in loans, and as a result spend the majority of your life paying back loans that you probably could have gone without. If the money you get in your refund greatly exceeds what you need after paying the bills and putting some away to save, then return what is left to reduce your loan obligation.

Getting a Job

Perhaps the money that you have coming in is not enough to pay the bills and provide for your family. That means that you may possibly have to find a job to help make ends meet.

If you do decide to get a job, try to find one that is willing to work with your schedule. If you cannot find a job that is willing to accommodate your needs, and have to take a job working odd hours, managing your time will become even more critical. Make sure you allocate sufficient study time as well as quality time with your child.

Chapter 6 Review

Points to Consider

♥ Learn to manage your money effectively by establishing a budget. Use your refund to pay your bills for the semester, and put away some into a savings account. If you still have a substantial amount of your refund remaining, consider returning those funds to reduce the amount of loans you will have to pay back later.

♥ If you have to work, try to find a job that will accommodate your schedule. If that is not possible, then be sure to manage your time even more closely.

Questions to Consider

1. Have you already established a budget for yourself? What money habits have you learned from your parents? Were they good habits? What would you do differently?

2. Will you have to take out loans for college? Have you applied for any scholarships?

3. Do you have plans to work while in college? Is it because you want to, or need to?

L.O.V.E. Activity

♥ Track your spending for a month. At the end of the month, take a look at your list. Identify the expenses that will occur monthly. Now take a look at the other expenses. Are they necessary expenses? Can you reduce them? Tally up the total, adjusting or removing any unnecessary expenses. Then add an additional twenty percent to the total to put away for savings. Make this your monthly budget, and try to stick to it as closely as possible. Re-examine your budget six months from now and make adjustments, if needed.

7. Developing Positive Parenting Habits

*L*iving in the south suburbs of Chicago, there aren't too many days that go by without hearing about a child being the victim of some senseless crime. Politicians, city officials, and other community and public organizations play the blame game, arguing about whether stricter gun laws should be applied. Others say more policing is needed, while some say that there needs to be more community programs and after-school activities. Honestly, I don't think that there is just one solution to the problem. I think it's a combination of all of the solutions. However, one of the most important solutions is the parent. As parents, we must instill important values and habits in our children while they are young, and they will keep those values with them as they grow older. Be a source of encouragement, love and empowerment for your child, and then he/she won't have to look to the streets for it.

Ensuring that your child grows up to be a productive part of society begins with you, and you must start now.

Creating a Routine

Kids thrive on structure. It is difficult to create a routine for everything you do; however, you should try to do it for the main tasks that you find yourself doing every day. Establish meal times so that your child will know when to expect to eat and you will reduce the number of times you hear, "Mommy, I'm hungry." Take notice of the time that your child gets irritable and cranky. That may be a sign that he/she is tired and needs to take a nap, which may also be time for you to get some things completed, or get in a nap yourself. Establish a bedtime for your child so that they can wake up ready for the day. Feel free to establish other routines during the day as needed, such as cleanup time, TV time, snack time, reading time, or outdoor time.

Healthy Eating Habits

With a hectic schedule of work and then school, I often found it a challenge to cook a healthy meal for my son. On many occasions, I would resort to making something quick like pizza or chicken nuggets, and always kept a supply of Kool-Aid and soda to drink. You could always find cookies or chips to snack on in my pantry, which my son often did. I noticed those bad habits began to take a toll on my son when he started putting on weight. I even put on weight myself.

Because of this, I knew that there were changes that I had to make. I stopped purchasing cookies, cut down on chips, and purchased granola bars and graham crackers to keep around the apartment as snacks. Instead of purchasing soda and Kool-Aid, I opted for healthier alternatives like one hundred percent juices and water. I would cook two to three times a week, making sure I cooked more than enough so that the next day we could eat leftovers. By incorporating these small changes, I soon began to notice both myself and my son losing the extra weight we put on.

The Value of Respect

I remember growing up, and not being allowed to call an adult by their first name, but had to address them as Mister or Misses. Then there was the rule of children not involving themselves in adult conversations, and only speaking when you are spoken to. Let's also not forget about remembering to say, "Please" and "Thank You." Respect is an important value that all kids need to learn. You may not have to follow all of the ways that were incorporated back in the day, however, make sure your child can distinguish the difference between a child and an adult. Teach them how to speak to adults respectfully, including yourself. Having a child at a young age, at times, can be difficult. Although you know you are not an adult, you must make sure that your child respects you as one. You cannot be their friend, and expect them to respect you as a parent. You must be able to discipline them when they are doing wrong, and praise them when they do right.

Furthermore, be sure to teach your child to respect other adults as well. Teach them how they should address adults, and be sure to correct their actions when they are behaving in a disrespectful manner towards an adult.

Quality Time

Your presence is one of the most important factors of parenting. Spending time with your child is important for their social and emotional development. You don't have to be a stay at home mom, or have to be around your child twenty-four hours a day. Everyone is entitled to some alone time every now and then. However, make sure that you always make time for your child. Before they go to bed, take a few minutes to read to them. Have conversations with your child asking them about their day, and encourage them to explain beyond just saying their day was "good." Take them out to eat, or to the park to play. Establish a family game or movie night. At the end of the day, it's not about how much you spend, or how extravagant of a place you go. It is about the memories and the time you spent with them, and those small moments will be what your child remembers and cherishes.

Be Your Child's Biggest Cheerleader

No one can encourage your child more than you can. They look to you for approval, and do things to get your attention, be it good or bad. Therefore, make sure you give your child lots of praise when they learn something new or do something good. That way, they will always strive to do what is good. If the only time you give them attention is when they do bad things, then they will continue to do those things because those are the only times that you seem to notice them.

Challenge your child to try new things, and encourage them when they are unsure. Your encouragement and support is important to them, and with it, they feel that they can conquer the world.

Introduce Positive Role Models and Activities

Surrounding your child with other positive role models gives them the opportunity to see other people doing good things. As a parent, it is difficult to expose your child to many different things on your own, simply because of the time required to do so.

Your local library or park district may have seasonal activities that your child can participate in. A lot of the activities are free, and can help your child explore their interests.

Check into any mentoring programs available in your area. If you don't have a male adult in the home, find a close male adult that you can trust, who is willing to spend time with your child. Having a healthy relationship with an adult male is important in your child's development, especially for boys. As moms, sometimes we overlook just how important interaction with male adults is to our children. Boys must know how to conduct themselves as young men, and they must see a man in order to be able to do so. Girls need to be able to have a healthy relationship with males as well.

Be the Example

Lastly, your child is your biggest fan. They will imitate the way you talk, dress, and interact with others. They are even watching and listening to you when you think that they are not. Therefore, be sure to be a positive example for your child. Be mindful of how you talk around them and to them. Show them how to be respectful to others by being respectful. Teach them love by showing it to them. Show them how to encourage others by encouraging them.

Chapter 7 Review

Points to Consider

- ♥ Kids thrive on structure. Make sure you establish a routine for your child.
- ♥ Teach your child healthy eating habits early; this will lead to a healthier life for them in the long run.
- ♥ Teaching your child to respect themselves and others will help them to have positive relationships with others as they grow older.
- ♥ Being present in your child's life is important. Make sure to set time aside to give them some one-on-one interaction with you.
- ♥ Encouraging your child and praising them when they do well is key to their confidence and motivation.
- ♥ Introduce positive role models and activities into your child's life so that they can be exposed to many things and discover their interests.
- ♥ Commit to being a positive example for your child.

Questions to Consider

1. What can you do to ensure your child eats healthier?

2. How do you teach your child respect?

3. What are some activities that you do with your child? How can you incorporate more quality time with your child into the day?

4. Does your child have any other positive role models in his/her life? What types of activities does your child like to participate in?

5. How can you be a positive role model for your child? What bad habits do you have that may not be a good influence? Which ones can you commit to eliminating now?

L.O.V.E. Activity

♥ It is very easy for us, as parents, to punish our children for bad behavior. However, we tend to overlook the moments when our children do good things. Being able to recognize those things start with changing our perspective. Begin a journal. Each day, no matter how bad the day may go, identify at least one good thing about your day and write it down. Then write down one goal to achieve for the following day.

8. Happily Ever After?

*A*fter I had my baby, I thought that my son's father and I would be together forever. I envisioned us moving in together and raising our son, and eventually getting married. Then, we would live happily ever after...or so I thought. I still had a lot to learn when it came to relationships, and this was just the beginning.

Understanding Relationships

Being committed to someone in a relationship is nothing to take lightly. When you are in a relationship with someone, you are creating a connection. At times, the connection can pose a risk to you and/or your dreams if the person you are pursuing a relationship with has completely different goals, or has no goals at all. Just like it is important to surround yourself with friends who are supportive, it is just as important to be sure that you enter a relationship with someone who shares the same goals as you, and who also has your best interests in mind. You should be able to see this in their words as well as their actions.

Love Is a Two-Way Street

You must be willing to give love to your partner just as much as you are willing to receive love from your partner. At times this may require you to make sacrifices. However, sacrifice does not mean that you allow your partner to mistreat or disrespect you. It means that you will have to communicate at times when you do not feel like talking, and continue to love them even if you do not like them at that moment. If you are not willing to reciprocate what you want to receive, then you may need to reconsider being in a relationship.

Is Marriage A Possibility?

When you marry someone, you are making a commitment to be with them for the rest of your life. You are agreeing to love them unconditionally, and committing to make things work, no matter how hard it gets. Marriage does not make relationships better; it is a commitment to make it work. Again, you want to be sure that you both share common goals and are both working in each other's best interest before making such a serious commitment.

While it is possible to have a loving and lasting marriage at such a young age, it is very difficult. When you are young, you both are growing emotionally and experiencing many things. The person you marry at 18 may not be the same person at 21, let alone 25. You will change as well. Being married means that you both accept that change and will stick with each other along the way.

Know Who You Are

Never go into a relationship expecting it to "complete" you. A relationship should not be what makes you happy. You should know who you are and be happy before you get into a relationship. A relationship should add to your happiness, and not be the source of it. By staying focused on pursuing your goals and working to achieve them, you will find your true happiness, and that will lead you to the type of relationship you desire.

Chapter 8 Review

Points to Consider

♥ Being in a relationship is nothing to take lightly. Make sure you enter into a relationship with someone who supports you and has your best interests in mind.

♥ Love is a two-way street. You must be willing to give love just as you are willing to receive it.

♥ Marriage means that you accept that person; you will love them unconditionally, and stick with each other even when things are not going well.

♥ Do not expect a relationship to make you happy. You must know who you are before pursuing a relationship.

Questions to Consider

1. Are you and your child's father still together? If so, are you both committed to each other? Are you considering marriage?

2. If you and your child's father are no longer together, why not? What lessons did you learn from the relationship? What did you learn about yourself?

3. Do you think you are ready to get married? Why or why not?

L.O.V.E. Activity

♥ Make a list of the goals you want to achieve. Next to each goal, write down how a relationship could negatively affect that goal. Finally, for each goal, write down how you would want your ideal partner to help or support you in achieving your goals.

9. After the Breakup

I was tired of fighting, and tired of trying to make things work. I had *walked* three miles from my house to his in an effort to save my relationship. I stood outside of his house, waiting for him to come out. Instead of coming out, he looked down at me from his window, and said he no longer wanted to be with me. At that moment, it felt like a dagger had been pierced into my stomach. As I looked up, I saw her staring through the window down at me, I thought to myself, *He chose her over me? What about us? What about our son?* I could not believe it. So many emotions overcame me at once. I felt rage, like a lioness trying to protect her den. Sadness, for what I knew would never be. Confusion and uncertainty of what led to this moment. Then, peace. I knew and trusted that whatever came next, I would be ok. He came outside and offered to give me a ride home. I reluctantly agreed.

Finding Closure

While in route to my house, he began to tell me how sorry he was and how much he loved me, but that he decided to be with her. They also had a child together. He went on to explain that she gave him an ultimatum: he had to be with her, or he would not see his daughter again, so he decided to be with her.

How could he expect me to understand? So what, she gave him an ultimatum, but what about us? What about *our* son?

As we continued to sit in the car, I knew it was time for me to move on. A part of me wanted to hold on to the hope that one day we would be together. However, there was another part inside of me that knew that I deserved better. Yes, he was trying to do right by his daughter, but it was at our expense. He would be able to see his daughter, but now my child and our relationship would be negatively impacted.

So my decision was made. It was time to move on. I told him that I was not okay with the situation. I asked him once more if he was sure about his decision because I knew that once I set foot out of the car, it was over for good. Once I walked away, there would be no turning back. He said he was sure. I kissed him goodbye, and that was the end of our relationship.

Although I was hurt, I was sure about my decision. I knew that anyone who was not able to put me and my son first in their lives did not deserve to be with me. I understood it was a difficult situation that he had been put in, but ultimately I had to do what was in the best interest of me and my child.

He Is Still Your Child's Father

My son's father was caught in a very difficult situation. He was forced to choose between a relationship and his child. This story is an unfortunate reality for many fathers. Regardless of how things ended between you and your child's father, you should never use your child as leverage or revenge against him. It is unfair to them both, and in the end it only ends up hurting the child. Furthermore, doing so will only yield the opposite result you desire. Using your child as leverage against the father will only push him further away, sometimes even to the point where he no longer tries to come around for your child.

Your job, now that the relationship is over, is to do what is in the best interest of your child, and unless your child's father is a threat to the well-being of your child, he should be a part of your child's life.

Closing the Door

After our breakup, my son's father remained a part of his life. However, I made it clear to him that our relationship was over, even our physical one. Just because we had a child did not mean that I was an easy target for him to have sex with.

It is important that once your relationship is over, you know your worth. Do not allow yourself to be taken advantage of by your ex simply because you have a child together, or because you were comfortable with him. If he does not value being in a relationship with you, then he should not be able to have sex with you. Furthermore, if the relationship is over, move on. Sex did not keep the relationship, and it definitely will not get it back.

Chapter 9 Review

Points to Consider

♥ Having closure after a breakup means forgiving the other person, and accepting the fact that the relationship is over.

♥ You should never use your child as leverage against the father. It only ends up hurting your child.

♥ If the relationship is over, do not allow yourself to be taken advantage of. Know your worth, and know that sex will neither keep nor get back a relationship.

Questions to Consider

1. Were there any unresolved issues between you and your child's father after the breakup? Were you able to remain friends?

2. Did the breakup affect your child's relationship with his/her father? Have you made it difficult for him to see your child? If so, why?

3. Are you and your child's father still having sex even though you two are no longer together? If so, why?

L.O.V.E. Activity

♥ In your journal, write about your breakup. Include what happened, how you felt, and what issues were left unresolved. What did you do in this relationship that you will do differently in your next one?

10. Learning to Forgive and Love Yourself Again

*M*y transition from being an honor student to becoming a teen mom took a toll on my self-confidence and self-esteem. I immediately switched from being an over-achieving, optimistic student, to being a realist who played it safe and did just enough to get by. That shift occurred because deep down inside, I felt that I had let myself down. I no longer felt that I could rely on myself to do things right. I did not understand how such a smart person could get caught up in a situation like I did. Me, a teenage mom? That was not supposed to happen. That did not happen to kids like me. No way – I was too smart to do that. It did not seem fair how I was the one that wound up pregnant. However, here I was – a young kid with a kid.

The looks of disappointment were not looks that I was used to. I was used to being the star student, great athlete, or over-achiever. I was not used to being rejected by friends or their parents. I was not used to being the one that kids were told not to hang out with.

I felt that I let everyone down, including myself. Everyone had great expectations of me, as did I. As a result, I allowed all of the feelings of rejection and disappointment to turn into anger. That anger drove me to prove everyone wrong, to prove that I could still make it in spite of what they thought. So, I worked hard and succeeded at completing my education, and yes, I proved them wrong! But now what? Here I was, successful, but there was still this anger inside me. Why was it still there?

It would take a few more years for me to finally realize why I was still so angry. I was no longer angry at those who doubted or rejected me. I was angry at myself. Only after I realized this, did my true healing begin.

Forgiving Yourself

Yes, you were brave enough to have your child at such a young age and care for him/her, but have you truly forgiven yourself for getting yourself in that position to begin with? Are you constantly thinking about how your life may have been if you made a different decision, or opted not to date your child's father? If so, then you still have not truly forgiven yourself.

Truly forgiving yourself means accepting the situation as it is, as well as the choices you have made, and moving forward. It is about no longer thinking about what may have been if you made a different decision. It is about making the best of your current situation, and not letting it be your excuse for failure. Everyone is entitled to making bad decisions from time to time, but the true test is in how you handle things after those decisions have been made. You must move forward, trust yourself to make better decisions in the future, and know that you can still make it.

Love Yourself Again

I did not realize how much having a baby at a young age truly affected me emotionally. Forgiving myself was only half the battle. The next step was learning to love myself again.

After having my son, I often had feelings of inadequacy. There were times when I felt no one would want to be in a relationship with me because I had a child. At times, I also felt that attaining the life that I wanted for me and my son was unrealistic. Because of these feelings, I would sometimes settle, both in my relationships and in my education/career.

Often, I would find myself in relationships that I knew were not good for me. However, even when I was dating a potentially great guy, I would often give him a false portrayal of myself by behaving in ways that I thought would make me more desirable to him. I felt that being myself wasn't good enough because I felt I was not good enough.

When it came to my education and career, I became so used to doing just enough to get by that I stopped putting in the effort to do things great and settled for average. I forgot how to really work hard to get what I wanted.

It was only after I sat back and examined my behavior that I realized that I was sabotaging my own success. Learning to love myself again meant that I needed to truly believe that I deserved to be happy. I deserved to be in a good relationship, I deserved to be successful, and I had to believe in myself enough to not be afraid to stand for and accomplish what I wanted.

Having a child does not mean that you have to settle for less in life. You must love yourself enough to know that your success is still attainable, and you are still worth that dream.

Chapter 10 Review

Points to Consider

♥ Truly forgiving yourself means to no longer dwell on what could have been and the choices you made, but to focus on what is, and move forward.

♥ Loving yourself means believing that you deserve to be happy, and going after what you want for your life.

Questions to Consider

1. Have you forgiven yourself for making bad choices? If not, what do you think you need to do in order to be able to forgive yourself?

2. Based on your actions, do you think that you love yourself? Why or why not?

L.O.V.E. Activity

♥ Write down a list of goals for yourself. Now look over them. Which goals are you actively pursuing? Are there any that you are not currently working on? If so, why not?

♥ Write an encouraging letter to yourself. Mention the things that you hope to achieve, as well as what you hope that you learn. List the things that you forgive yourself for. Keep the letter and refer back to it when you are feeling uncertain or just need to hear an encouraging word from yourself.

11. Protecting Yourself and Your Future

You know from having a child how much more difficult it has become to pursue your dreams. Because of this, you want to minimize the chance of any other obstacles getting in your way. Taking proactive steps to protect yourself and your future is the one way to help minimize those unexpected bumps in the road.

Practice Safe Sex

If after having your child, you decide that sex is not something you will have again until you are married, then that is great! Abstinence is the best way to prevent future unwanted pregnancies and sexually transmitted diseases. However, chances are that now that you are sexually active, you may engage in sexual activity again. If that is the case, then you want to protect yourself from getting pregnant again, and from contracting STD's, by practicing safe sex. Talk to your doctor or visit your local health clinic to discuss birth control options.

Remember, you now have someone else who depends on you and who will also be affected by the decisions you make. Therefore, do not place your life in someone else's hands! Sex is not always a planned activity, and because of this, you must be ready to protect yourself at all times. Keep condoms on hand. Some colleges and universities give condoms to students for free; so check with the nurse on your college campus for information on contraception as well.

Finally, never trust using the pull-out method. You still can get pregnant, and you are completely unprotected from contracting an STD.

Avoid Drugs and Alcohol

Everyday we hear about the effects of drugs and alcohol. Protect your future by staying away from them. Using drugs and alcohol not only has a negative effect on your health, but as a teen and a parent, it can also lead to serious legal consequences. Therefore, make sure that you do not allow people who indulge in drugs or alcohol in your home or around your child. Their actions can endanger the safety of you and your child, and you risk losing custody of your child if they get caught while you and/or your child are around.

Choose Your Friends Wisely

You know the things that you want to achieve for yourself. Therefore, it is important that you surround yourself with friends who also are working towards positive goals. Not everyone wants to see you succeed, or has your best interests in mind, so it is important that you know who your true friends are. Associate yourself with people who will encourage you, push you to do better, and most importantly, be honest with you. You need to know when you are doing great as well as if you are losing focus, and only friends who truly want to see you succeed will tell you those things.

Chapter 11 Review

Points to Consider

♥ Practice safe sex to avoid any future unplanned pregnancies and to prevent STD's. Do not put your life in someone else's hands - keep your own supply of condoms on hand.

♥ Avoid alcohol and drugs and never allow it in your home or around you and your child

♥ Choose your friends wisely. Surround yourself with friends who will be honest with you and have your best interests in mind.

Questions to Consider

1. Are you practicing abstinence? If not, what are you doing to prevent getting pregnant again or contracting STD's?

2. How do you think taking drugs or alcohol can affect you and your child's future? How do you resist the pressure to indulge?

3. Are your current friends supportive of your goals? If not, how do you deal with that?

L.O.V.E. Activity

♥ Expanding your network of positive people is important to your success. Find a local support group for teen moms. Contact them and ask about their program. If they have an office, go visit them and learn more.

12. Setting Your Vision in Motion

*G*raduating from college was one of my greatest achievements. I beat the odds of being a teenage mom doomed to live in poverty and rely on welfare to provide for my needs. I was one step closer to reaching my dreams, and being able to give my son the life he deserved.

I earned my degree. It was up to me to put it to use. However, as the time drew closer for me to transition into the workforce, I was uncertain about what to do next.

I graduated in May 2001. However, three months later, I still had not been able to secure a job. Interview after interview, it all came down to one basic fact – I did not have the experience. Nevertheless, I remained persistent and continued to apply for jobs that I qualified for.

Just when I thought things were looking hopeful, another obstacle presented itself. It was September. I was back at home with my mom, and looked for work steadily. I made plans to go back to my alma mater to attend a career fair. Many companies were expected to be in attendance, so I knew my chances of landing a job were high.

So, I got on the road and headed to the career fair. I was no more than thirty minutes away, when breaking news interrupted the radio station, stating that one of the Twin Towers in New York was hit by a plane. The date was September 11, 2001.

When I arrived at the career fair, it looked like a ghost town. After the planes hit the towers, downtown Chicago was evacuated as a safety precaution. As a result, only a few companies scheduled to be at the career fair showed up.

So, it was back to the drawing board. Still, I refused to give up. I began to read articles on how other inexperienced workers were able to tap into the workforce. I used the advice and applied for other positions within my area of focus. As a result, I landed a job and there began my career in the IT industry.

Setting your Vision in Motion

Congratulations to you! You have achieved a major accomplishment of earning your degree, and doing it while caring for a child. Now it is time to start marketing yourself.

On occasion, fear may try to sneak in and make you doubt your abilities. However, that is when you must realize that you are truly capable of achieving your dreams. The path to success is not smooth, so expect a few obstacles. Just remember to be persistent and stay focused, and success will surely come your way.

There is nothing holding you back now but yourself. Let go of any doubts, any fears, and any uncertainties and continue to move forward. Once you establish your momentum, you will be able to look back at all of your successes, and truly know that you are capable of accomplishing anything. See you at the top!

Chapter 12 Review

Points to Consider

- ♥ Do not allow fear to cause you to doubt your abilities.
- ♥ The path to success is not smooth. There will be obstacles that you may encounter. However, staying persistent and focused is the key to your success.

Questions to Consider

1. Now that you have your degree, what are you going to do with it? Have you already secured a job?
2. What goals do you have for you and your child in this next chapter of your life? What do you have to do in order to achieve those goals?

L.O.V.E. Activity

♥ In order to continue to succeed, you must continue to dream. A vision board is a tool used to provide clarity to your dreams. Create a vision board. Get a large poster board and some old magazines. Cut out pictures, words, and phrases that reflect your vision for all aspects of your life and glue them to the poster board. When complete, hang it on your wall as a daily reminder. Feel free to add to it as well. Which vision on your board will you achieve next?

Resources

ACT/SAT

- ♥ http://www.act.org
- ♥ http://sat.collegeboard.org/

Childcare

- ♥ http://childcare.gov/
- ♥ http://eclkc.ohs.acf.hhs.gov/hslc/HeadStartOffices

Financial Assistance

- ♥ http://www.acf.hhs.gov/programs/css
- ♥ https://www.acf.hhs.gov/programs/ocs/resource/liheap-brochures
- ♥ http://www.benefits.gov

Financial Aid for College

- ♥ http://www.fafsa.ed.gov

GED Information

- ♥ http://www.passged.com

Housing

- ♥ www.hud.gov/progdesc/voucher.cfm
- ♥ http://portal.hud.gov/hudportal/HUD?src=/topics/rental _assistance

Medical Insurance

- ♥ http://www.medicaid.gov/index.html
- ♥ http://www.insurekidsnow.gov/state/index.html

Organizations/Programs

- ♥ http://advocatesforadolescentmothers.com
- ♥ http://www.dhs.state.il.us/page.aspx?item=30518
- ♥ http://newmomsinc.org/

Scholarships

- ♥ http://www.fastweb.com
- ♥ http://www.scholarships.com
- ♥ http://www.finaid.org/scholarships

About the Author

Born in the south suburbs of Chicago, Alicia T. Bowens learned the meaning of perseverance at a very young age. Alicia became a teenage mother during her sophomore year of high school at the age of fifteen; however she didn't let that stop her from pursuing her dreams.

Immediately after high school, Alicia went on to attend the University of Illinois at Urbana-Champaign, taking her then three-year old son with her. She graduated in 2001, receiving her Bachelors of Science degree in Business Administration/MIS and soon after obtained a position in the IT industry.

In 2005, Alicia went on to obtain her MBA and M.S. in Information Systems Management from Keller Graduate School.

Alicia is a lifetime member of the National Black MBA Association, Chicago Chapter, having served on the Executive Board and Marketing & Communications Committee from 2006-2010. She also participated in the Leaders Of Tomorrow (LOT) program, a mentoring program for high school students. Alicia has also been involved in other teen mentoring programs, such as The Legacy Initiative and Y.Our Time Is Now (YTIN), and has done multiple speaking engagements at area high schools on college and career planning, as well as sharing her experiences of being a teenage mother.

In 2010, Alicia became a certified life coach. As a life coach, it is her desire to share her experiences - both successes and failures - in an effort to empower others to achieve their goals, despite the obstacles that may present themselves in life. From April 2011 through December 2012, Alicia co-hosted a weekly radio show titled "The L.O.V.E. Perspective," which focused on empowering and motivating others to live their dreams and improve their lives.

For More Information, or to book for workshops and speaking engagements, please contact:

Alicia Bowens
P.O. Box 434
Matteson, IL 60443

Phone: 855.ALI.CIA1 (855.254.2421)
Email: livingdreams@aliciabowens.com
Website: www.aliciabowens.com

CPSIA information can be obtained at www.ICGtesting.com
Printed in the USA
LVOW04s1533240814

400622LV00003B/298/P